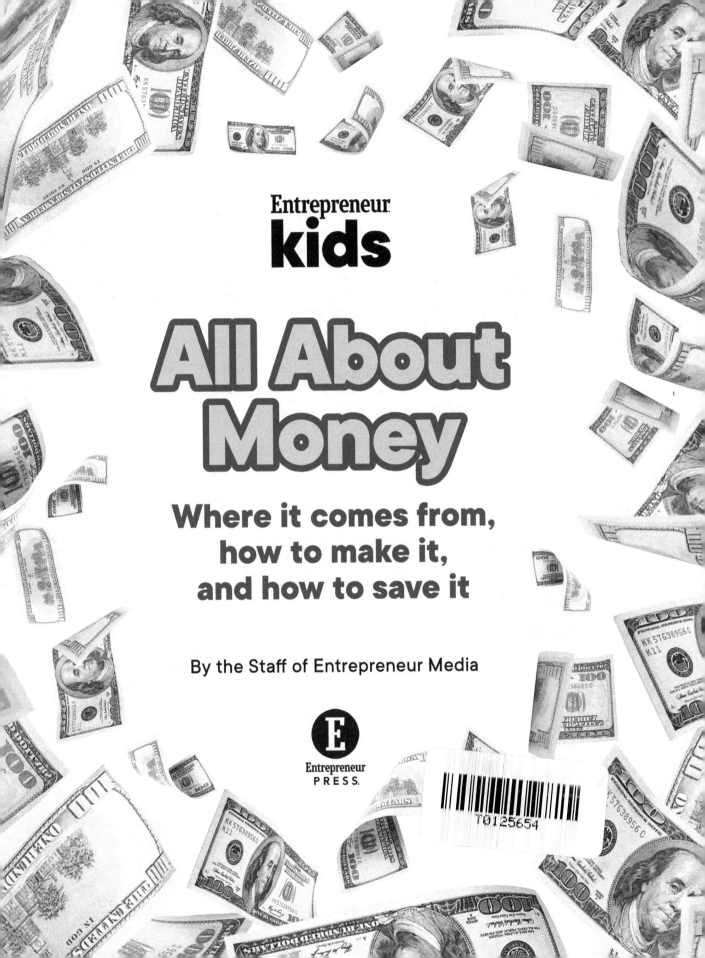

Entrepreneur
kids

All About Money

Where it comes from, how to make it, and how to save it

By the Staff of Entrepreneur Media

E

Entrepreneur
P R E S S.

T0125654

Entrepreneur Press, Publisher
Cover Design: Andrew Welyczko
Production and Composition: AbandonedWest Creative, Inc.

An application to register this book for cataloging has been submitted to the Library of Congress.

ISBN 978-1-64201-139-5 (paperback) | ISBN 978-1-61308-452-6 (ebook)

Printed in the United States of America

25 24 23 22 21 10 9 8 7 6 5 4 3 2 1

References

Albertyn, Diana. "The Ultimate 101 List of SA Business Ideas to Get You Started." *Entrepreneur Magazine*, Irvine, CA. www.entrepreneur.com/article/327572

Entrepreneur Staff. "How to Write a Business Plan." Entrepreneur Magazine, Irvine, CA. www.entrepreneur.com/article/247575

Neilson, Amy Rauch. "What's So Great About Being Your Own Boss?" *Entrepreneur Magazine*, Irvine, CA. www.entrepreneur.com/article/50944

Felber, Josh. "5 Lessons from Kid Entrepreneurs Making More Money Than You." *Entrepreneur Magazine*, Irvine, CA. www.entrepreneur.com/article/282686

Herzog, Kenny. "These 13-Year-Old Board Game Creators Can Teach All Entrepreneurs a Thing or Two" *Entrepreneur Magazine*, Irvine, CA. www.entrepreneur.com/article/352194

Image Credits

FC   LightField Studios/Shutterstock.com
i   MVelishchuk/Shutterstock.com
2   James Steidl/Shutterstock.com
3   Kapustin Igor/Shutterstock.com
3   Everett Collection/Shutterstock.com
4   Siberian Art/Shutterstock.com
4   pixs4u/Shutterstock.com
5   Lucky-photographer/Shutterstock.com
6   Somchai Som/Shutterstock.com
7   nimon/Shutterstock.com
7   Valerii_Dex/Shutterstock.com
8   Zelfit/Shutterstock.com
8   ILYA AKINSHIN/Shutterstock.com
9   FrameAngel/Shutterstock.com
10   unverdorben jr/Shutterstock.com
11   tony4urban/Shutterstock.com
12   New Africa/Shutterstock.com
12   vkilikov/Shutterstock.com
12   Frederic Muller/Shutterstock.com
12   kamui29/Shutterstock.com
12   Pla2na/Shutterstock.com

12   eivanov/Shutterstock.com
12   WorldStock/Shutterstock.com
12   VAKS-Stock Agency/Shutterstock.com
14   B. Melo/Shutterstock.com
14   SiAna/Shutterstock.com
15   Martina_L/Shutterstock.com
15   tofang/Shutterstock.com
18   Prostock-studio/Shutterstock.com
19   artboySHF/Shutterstock.com
20   Pixel-Shot/Shutterstock.com
21   Pixel-Shot/Shutterstock.com
25   New Africa/Shutterstock.com
26   FrameStockFootages/Shutterstock.com
27   lunamarina/Shutterstock.com
28   In Green/Shutterstock.com
29   Olena Yakobchuk/Shutterstock.com
32   Anna Timokhina/Shutterstock.com
33   ImageFlow/Shutterstock.com
34   mervas/Shutterstock.com
35   MicrostockStudio/Shutterstock.com
36   mervas/Shutterstock.com

39   Image courtesy of Scott Brown
42   Fab_1/Shutterstock.com
43   Cheryl Casey/Shutterstock.com
44   My Life Graphic/Shutterstock.com
45   Kingsman Asset/Shutterstock.com
46   Amirul Syaidi/Shutterstock.com
47   Ljupco Smokovski/Shutterstock.com
48   Uncle Leo/Shutterstock.com
50   Africa Studio/Shutterstock.com
51   hedgehog94/Shutterstock.com
52   Jenn Huls/Shutterstock.com
53   RomanYa/Shutterstock.com
53   nikiteev_konstantin/Shutterstock.com
54   YinYang/iStockPhoto.com

Illustrations on FC, 2, 3, 4, 6, 7, 9, 10, 13, 16, 17, 21, 23, 24, 26, 27, 29, 34, 37, 41, 44, 46, 47, 49, 51, 53, 55, 56 by Carolyn Williams

Additional illustrations by Andrew Welyczko

Entrepreneur kids

Contents
all about money

WHERE DOES *money* COME FROM?

What is Bartering?

Have you ever traded food at lunch? Let's say you want cookies, but all you have for a snack is chips. And then you see a friend has cookies, so you ask her if you can trade snacks. This is called **bartering** and that's exactly what people used to do before money was invented. Only back then, instead of chips and cookies, people were trading cows for goats or chickens for pigs. Whatever was traded, it had to be something that both people agreed upon—and equal enough so both people felt they were getting a fair deal.

Over time, people got tired of always trading goods, so coins were invented. The very first coins were just pieces of silver or gold. They weren't perfectly round and they didn't all look the same. But then, in about the 600s B.C., the kingdom of Lydia (now Turkey) began to make coins from silver and gold, called **electrum**.

Did You Know?

The first nickels were much smaller. They were called "half dimes" and weighed exactly half as much as a dime.

Did You Know?

Alexander Hamilton is the only person to be featured on some form of U.S. currency since it was first printed in 1861. Before landing on the $10 bill in 1928, he appeared on seven different denominations!

Trading Notes for Coins

Governments and people continued to use coins to pay for things for many years. The first type of paper money was used in China more than 1000 years ago. This paper money was usually just a written promise to pay for something with gold or silver.

Have you ever written a note to or texted a friend to say, "If you give me your pack of gum, I'll bring you 50 cents tomorrow"? Well, that's similar to how early paper money was used. The paper itself wasn't worth a lot. It was the promise of the gold or silver that was valuable.

In the United States, paper money—like we know it today—wasn't used until the Civil War. President Abraham Lincoln issued the first one-dollar bill in 1862. The first dollar bill was much larger than the ones we use today and it had a portrait of Salmon P. Chase, the Secretary of the Treasury, at the time.

It wasn't until 1869 that the government decided to change the design of the dollar bill. They reduced the size of it by 30 percent, and they changed the picture to George Washington. They also added security features to the bill so people couldn't copy it or make fake money.

Keep Reading! →

Salmon P. Chase was originally on the one-dollar bill.

THE evolution OF MONEY

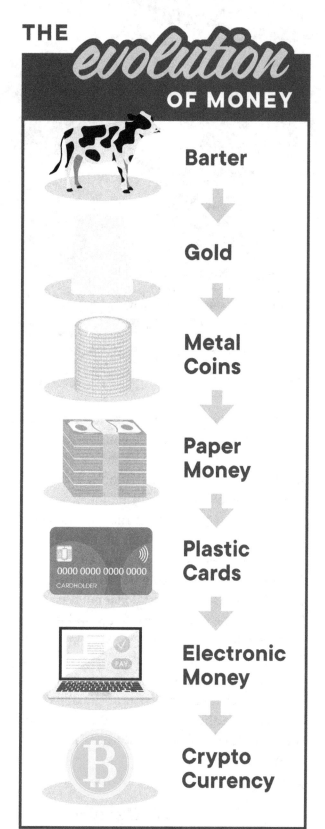

Barter

↓

Gold

↓

Metal Coins

↓

Paper Money

↓

Plastic Cards

↓

Electronic Money

↓

Crypto Currency

Coins, Change, Paper Money, Currency, Notes—Oh My!

People use many different words for money. Coins are often referred to as **change**. Has anyone ever asked you if you have any change? What they're really asking you for are coins. Pennies, nickels, dimes, and quarters are the most common types of coins. Half dollars and dollar coins are still made, but they are not used as often as the other coins. In fact, when many people come across a half dollar or a dollar coin, they often save it. Sometimes this is the beginning of their coin collection!

Paper money has many different names. **Currency**, or **legal tender**, are other names for money that is legally accepted by a country. In the U.S., the legal tender is dollars. Paper money is sometimes referred to as **notes** because all U.S. money are Federal Reserve Notes. Some of the more common terms for paper money are **cash** or **bills**. You may even hear people call money **greenbacks**. Greenbacks were the name for paper money during the Civil War. The name comes from the color of the bills, which had a green back. ⓚ

Did You Know?

The $100-dollar bill is sometimes called a **C-note**. "C" is for the Roman numeral 100. It's also sometimes called a "Benjamin" after Benjamin Franklin, who is pictured on the money.

HOW IS MONEY *made?*

The U.S. Mint

Coins and currency are actually made in different places. To learn about coins, let's take a look at the U.S. Mint.

The U.S. Mint was created in 1792 as the official place to make U.S. coins. Located in Philadelphia, the Mint made silver half dimes and copper cents. As the United States grew, so did the need for coins. More U.S. Mint locations were opened in:

- **Denver, Colorado**
- **Fort Knox, Kentucky**
- **San Francisco, California**
- **Washington, D.C.**
- **West Point, New York**

Today, you can take a tour of the Philadelphia or Denver Mint to see how coins are made.

Besides making the coins we use today, the U.S. Mint also creates collectible coins. Have you ever looked at the back of your quarters? Many of them have different states. You can start your own coin collection by finding quarters with each of the 50 states!

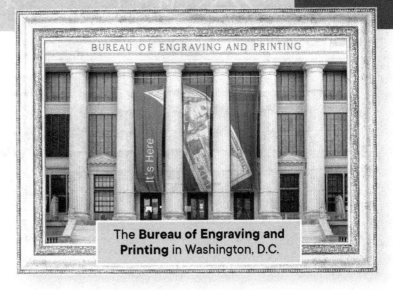

The **Bureau of Engraving and Printing** in Washington, D.C.

The U.S. Bureau of Engraving and Printing

Paper money (notes) are created and printed at the U.S. Department of Treasury's Bureau of Engraving and Printing. More $1 bills are made than any other denomination. Today there are seven different denominations printed: $1, $2, $5, $10, $20, $50, and $100. At one time there were also $500, $1000, $5000, and $10,000 bills, but they were discontinued in 1969 because not many people used them.

The largest bill ever printed was the $100,000 Gold Certificate. It was printed in 1934 and 1935 and was only used for transactions by the Federal Reserve Bank.

Decoding Coins

OBVERSE (HEADS)

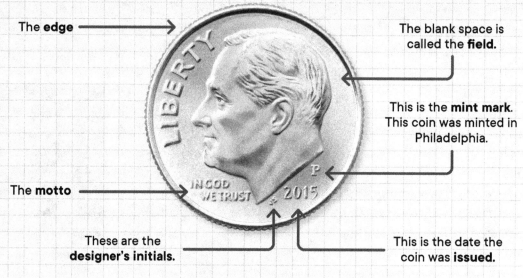

The **edge**

The blank space is called the **field.**

This is the **mint mark**. This coin was minted in Philadelphia.

The **motto**

These are the **designer's initials.**

This is the date the coin was **issued.**

REVERSE (TAILS)

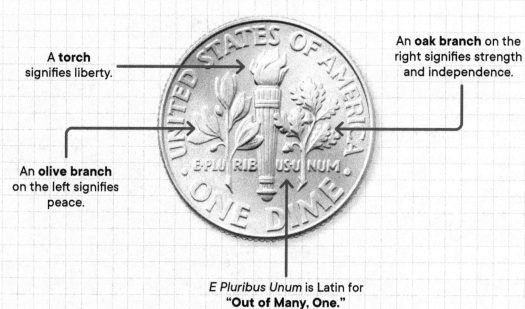

A **torch** signifies liberty.

An **oak branch** on the right signifies strength and independence.

An **olive branch** on the left signifies peace.

E Pluribus Unum is Latin for **"Out of Many, One."**

Decoding The Dollar Bill

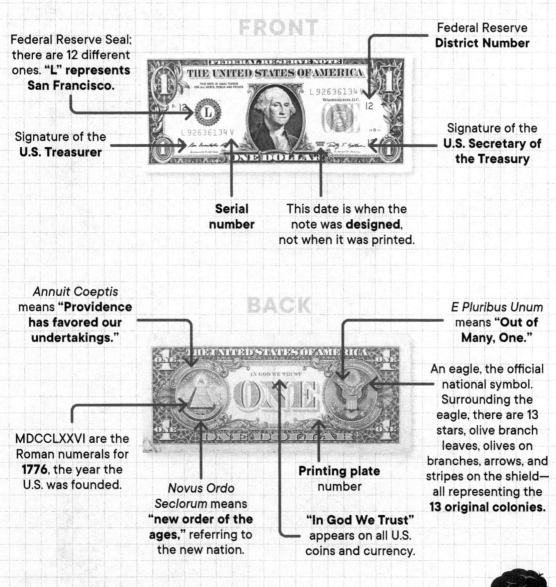

FRONT

Federal Reserve Seal; there are 12 different ones. **"L" represents San Francisco.**

Federal Reserve **District Number**

Signature of the **U.S. Treasurer**

Signature of the **U.S. Secretary of the Treasury**

Serial number

This date is when the note was **designed**, not when it was printed.

BACK

Annuit Coeptis means **"Providence has favored our undertakings."**

E Pluribus Unum means **"Out of Many, One."**

An eagle, the official national symbol. Surrounding the eagle, there are 13 stars, olive branch leaves, olives on branches, arrows, and stripes on the shield— all representing the **13 original colonies.**

MDCCLXXVI are the Roman numerals for **1776**, the year the U.S. was founded.

Novus Ordo Seclorum means **"new order of the ages,"** referring to the new nation.

Printing plate number

"In God We Trust" appears on all U.S. coins and currency.

Did You Know?

Have you ever wondered what the story is behind the dollar bill in your wallet? Where has it been? Who had it before you? You can go to **wheresgeorge.com** to see the history behind your dollar bill. And what's even more fun, you can track where your dollar bill goes *after* you spend it!

Design Your Own Currency

If you could design your own money, what would you include on it? Who would you feature? **Use these templates to draw your own money!**

Why Is Hamilton on a $10 Bill?

Alexander Hamilton was the first United States Secretary of the Treasury. He was appointed by President George Washington in 1789. Hamilton asked Congress to establish a national bank and the U.S. Mint. He has appeared on more denominations of money than any other person since 1861. He and Benjamin Franklin are the only non-presidents to have their portraits on currency.

What Is Interest?

Interest is money. If you have a savings account, your bank will give you money—called interest—for having that account. Besides paying you interest for your savings account, banks will also charge you interest if you take out a loan. If you take out a really big loan to buy a house or car, the bank will make a lot of money in interest in the time it takes you to pay it off.

What Is a Salary?

A **salary** is the amount of money your employer agrees to pay you to do your job. A salary is based on many things, such as your education level and your years of experience.

What Is Minimum Wage?

When most people get their first job, they are paid minimum wage. **Minimum wage** is the least amount of money that a company can pay you and it is often different depending on where you live. The federal minimum wage is $7.25—this means that no matter where you live, you shouldn't make less than $7.25 an hour. Many states have increased this amount so people have more money to pay their bills. When it is time for you to get a job, be sure to look up what minimum wage is in your area.

What Are Bitcoins?

Bitcoins are a new type of digital currency that were invented in 2008. They are not printed like dollars. They are online money. Bitcoins are made by computers using free software and held electronically in programs called "wallets." The future of bitcoins is uncertain because governments are worried about their lack of control over the currency.

Alexander Hamilton as he appears on the $10 bill.

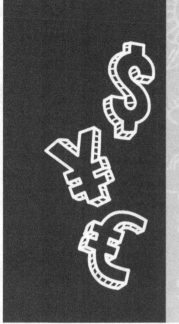

$ is money THE SAME IN EVERY COUNTRY?

Most countries have different names for their currency. Each country has a central bank that oversees their currency. Even though some countries share the same name for their money, their currencies are not usually the same. Check out this chart to see the different names for our world's currency!

Did You Know?

In the U.S., money is green, but the rest of the world uses many different colors!

COUNTRY	CURRENCY
Afghanistan	Afghani
Albania	Lek
Algeria, Iraq, Jordan, Kuwait, Libya, Serbia, Tunisia	Dinar
Angola	Kwanza
Argentina, Chile, Colombia, Cuba, Mexico, Philippines, Uruguay	Peso
Armenia	Dram
Aruba	Florin
Austria, Belgium, Cyprus, Estonia, Finland, France, Germany, Greece, Ireland, Italy, Latvia, Lithuania, Luxembourg, Malta, Netherlands, Portugal, Slovakia, Slovenia, Spain	Euro
Azerbaijan	Manat

COUNTRY	CURRENCY
Belarus	**Rubel**
Benin, Cameroon, French Polynesia, Gabon, Liechtenstein, Mali, Switzerland	**Franc**
Botswana	**Pula**
Brazil	**Rea**
Bulgaria	**Lev**
Cambodia	**Riel**
China	**Yuan**
Croatia	**Kuna**
Czech Republic	**Koruna**
Denmark	**Krone**
Egypt	**Egyptian Pound**
Ethiopia	**Birr**
Guatemala	**Quetzal**

COUNTRY	CURRENCY
India, Mauritius, Nepal, Pakistan, Seychelles	**Rupee**
Indonesia	**Rupiah**
Iran	**Rial**
Israel	**Sheqel**
Japan	**Yen**
Laos	**Kip**
Mongolia	**Tugrik**
Nigeria	**Naira**
Norway	**Krone**
Romania	**Leu**
Saudi Arabia	**Riyal**
Sweden	**Krona**
Thailand	**Baht**
United Kingdom	**Pound Sterling**

Match The Money

Can you guess which money goes with which country? Write the letter of the currency next to its country below. Hint: Some of the money is accepted in more than one country!

A

B

C

D

E

F

G

_____ CHINA

_____ FRANCE

_____ JAPAN

_____ MEXICO

_____ NIGERIA

_____ SERBIA

_____ UNITED KINGDOM

ANSWER KEY ON PAGE 55

Entrepreneur

word search

Find the words that are hidden in the puzzle. Words may be forward, backward, horizontal, vertical, or diagonal.

```
C W N W C B J Y O C Y N
J R A I D H R S U O O B
E G E P L A A R M I T A
E T W D L K R S T S R R
O M O A I E N A E D A T
R D S N N T N A V E D E
A X S C Q I C I R A E R
L Z Y F M U E A Y F H I
L A M O N E Y N R F V N
O O N I O C O H D D E G
D E I F N O T L I M A H
D N U M I S M A T I S T
```

CURRENCY	WAGE	BARTERING	DENOMINATION
MONEY	HAMILTON	TRADE	CREDIT CARD
DOLLAR	FRANKLIN	COIN	NUMISMATIST
SALARY	CHASE	NOTE	

ANSWER KEY ON PAGE 55

MONEY ORIGAMI *plane*

Follow the directions to fold a dollar bill into a paper airplane.

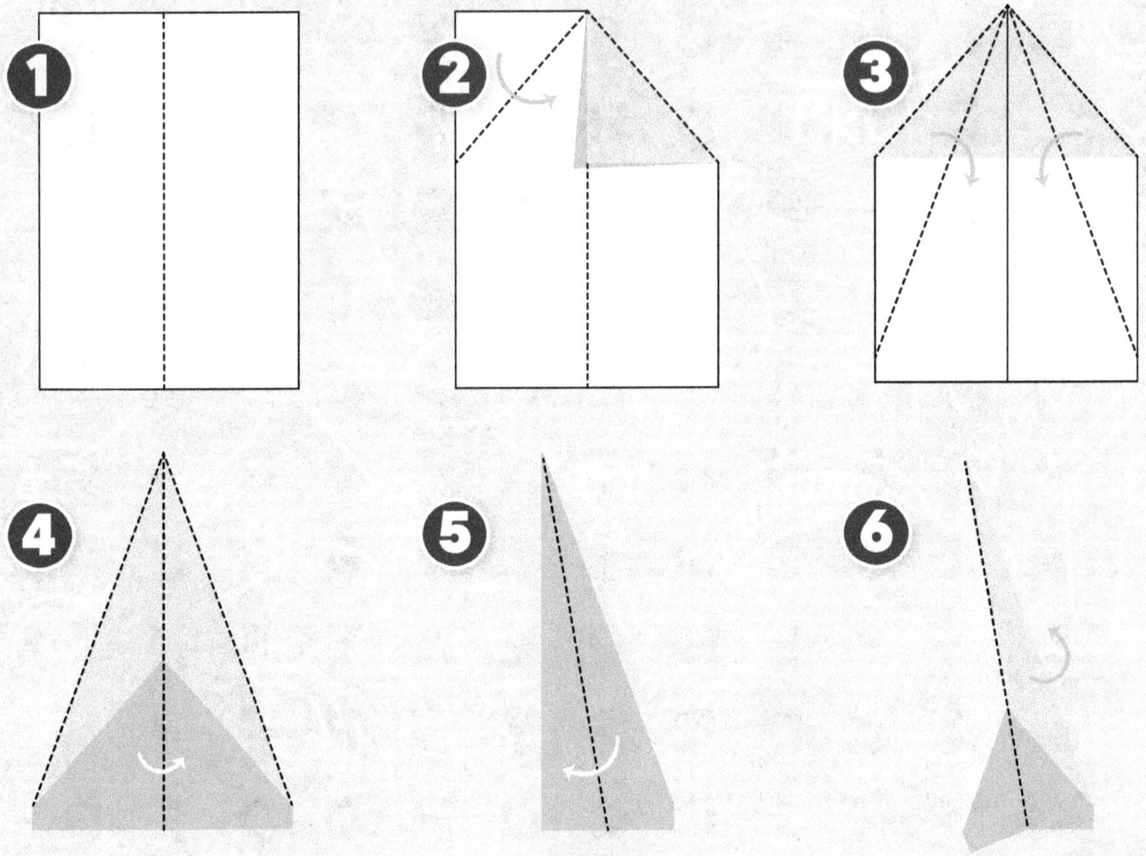

1

2

3

4

5

6

finished!

MONEY ORIGAMI *heart*

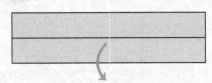

Follow the directions to fold a dollar bill into a heart.

1
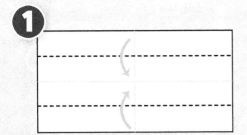

2
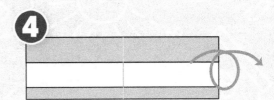

3

4

5
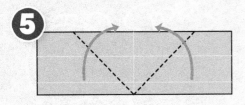

6
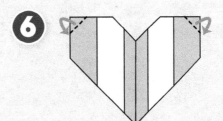

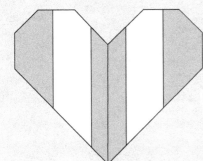

finished!

DREAMING ABOUT *money*

If you could go on a $1,000 shopping spree, where would you want to go? What would you buy? Who would you take with you?

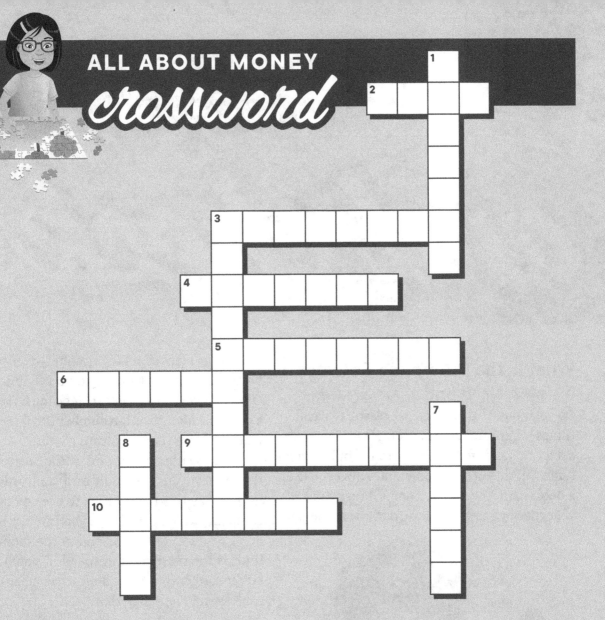

ACROSS

2. Another word for borrowing money.

3. When you get a job, you can get a ____ account.

4. Something you should do with your money.

5. Credit cards will charge you ____ if you don't pay your bill in full every month.

6. Before you buy something, you should know your ____.

9. ____ is on the dollar bill.

10. Another word for taking money out of your savings account.

DOWN

1. Banks will pay you interest on your ____ account.

3. You need to be 18 in order to get a ____.

7. In the U.S., the first one had a picture of Samuel P. Chase on it.

8. ____ come from the U.S. Mint.

ANSWER KEY ON PAGE 55

CREDIT CARDS, DEBIT CARDS, and checks

What Is the Difference Between a Debit Card and a Credit Card?

Do you know that you can use plastic to pay for things? There are two kinds of "plastic" money: debit cards and credit cards. They might look the same, but they are very different. When you use a **debit card**, the money comes directly out of your checking account. If you don't have enough money in your checking account, you won't be able to buy anything with your debit card. Often, you need to have a secret code known as a **personal identification number (PIN)** to enter when you use your debit card at stores.

When you use a **credit card**, you are borrowing the money from the credit card company. You have to pay this money back to the credit card company, which will charge you interest if you don't pay it in full at the end of the month. A **limit** is the most you can spend. If you have a credit card with a $500 limit, that means you can't spend more than that.

What Is a Check?

A **check** is a way to pay for things and a way to receive money. The money you spend with a personal check comes out of your checking account. The money you receive when someone pays you with a check is deposited into your bank account when you sign the back of the check and take it to the bank for deposit. For example, if Aunt Kate gives you a check for $25 for your birthday, in order to actually receive that $25, you need to go to the bank and either cash it, which means the bank will take the signed check and then give you $25, or you can deposit the money directly into your savings account.

Checks are also a way for companies to pay you for your work—this is called a **paycheck**. When you have a job, you will also need to have a checking and a savings account at a bank. This way, when you get your paycheck, you can deposit some of your money into your savings account and then some of your money into your checking account.

A few years ago, having a checking account was the only way to pay for things. People wrote personal checks for all sorts of things—groceries, clothes, and for fun things like sporting events and concerts.

As technology changed, so did the way people bank. Personal checks are no longer the only way to pay for things out of your checking account. Checks are still important, though. And at some point, you will probably need to know how to fill one out. Here is a sample check. Practice filling it in! ⓚ

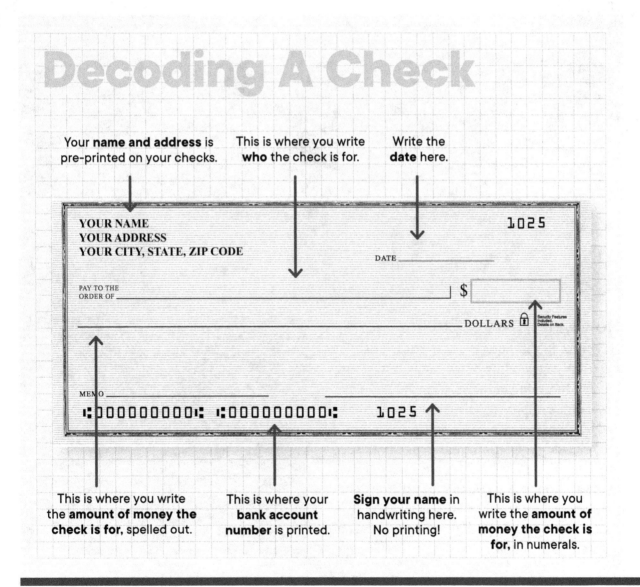

Decoding A Check

Your **name and address** is pre-printed on your checks.

This is where you write **who** the check is for.

Write the **date** here.

YOUR NAME
YOUR ADDRESS
YOUR CITY, STATE, ZIP CODE

1025

DATE _____

PAY TO THE ORDER OF _____

$ _____

_____ DOLLARS

Security Features Included. Details on Back.

MEMO _____

⑆000000000⑆ ⑆000000000⑆ 1025

This is where you write the **amount of money the check is for,** spelled out.

This is where your **bank account number** is printed.

Sign your name in handwriting here. No printing!

This is where you write the **amount of money the check is for,** in numerals.

let's make SOME MONEY

How Much Do People Make?

Having a job is how you get paid. Jobs pay differently depending on where you live, how much education you have, and who you work for. For example, a hairdresser may make $30,000 when they are just starting out, but if they decide to open up their own salon, they could make a lot more! A police officer may make an average of $54,155, but if they work hard and get promotions, they can make three times that! Here are a few examples of what different jobs can pay:

Elementary Teacher	$43,000
Dentist	$174,110
Registered Nurse	$73,418
Police Officer	$54,155
Surgeon	$255,110
Lawyer	$144,230
Hairdresser	$30,113
Illustrator	$40,000
Make-Up Artist	$46,000
Orthodontist	$225,760
Firefighter	$73,860

DO YOU WANT TO BE
your own boss?

Being your own boss is fun, but it's also a lot of work! Setting your own hours, giving yourself a raise when business is going well—all while working hard to do a job you love—is fun! It doesn't get any better than that, right?

Some  Advice from Young Entrepreneurs

Many people love being in business for themselves and wouldn't have it any other way. Not only do they call the shots, but, as young entrepreneurs, they're also getting a head start on what it takes to be a business success.

Flex Time Rules!

One of the biggest plusses to being a young entrepreneur is getting to be your own boss. "There are advantages to having your own business," says Keith Dixon, the 19-year-old owner of Golden Touch Car Wash in Pembroke Pines, Florida. "You can control how many hours you work, how much money you want to make, and who will work for you."

Dixon makes house calls to wash his customers' cars, vans, and RVs. His business is

Keep Reading! →

Did You Know?

An **entrepreneur** is a person who starts their own business.

21

a hit in his South Florida hometown, where the sun always shines and people want their cars to look good.

Getting Experience

Being a young entrepreneur also gives you a head start in the basics of running a business. Regina Jackson, owner of Regina's Jewelry Designs in Washington, DC, learned about setting prices and making her products better. After researching her competitors, Regina, then 16, realized she wasn't charging enough for her earrings, bracelets, and necklaces.

Jackson also focused on making her products stronger. "My jewelry has gotten better than it used to be," she says. "Now I use fishing line instead of string, and it's much better."

Ouch! That Hurts!

As with any pursuit in life, there are pitfalls to watch out for along the way. Jayson Meyer, 19, has what every young entrepreneur dreams of—a company worth six figures and a big office with a view of Daytona Beach, Florida. But it hasn't always been easy.

Meyer's hardest lesson came when a business partner he had trusted with a new project tried to pull a fast one and start a competing business.

Being a young entrepreneur calls for tough skin and a quick mind. These days, Meyer often consults with his greatest mentor, his father, for advice.

No doubt about it, there's a lot to be said for starting a business. Not only do you get to make your own hours and call the shots, but you're also well on your way to making your dreams become a reality. And no matter what path you choose down the road, having experience under your belt can only work to your advantage. Studies show that people who dabble in business as kids are more successful as adults. So, what are you waiting for?

what kind of job...

DO YOU WANT?

It's never too early to start thinking about your future. What do you see yourself doing in the future? Do you want to work with people? Or do you prefer working by yourself? Most importantly, what makes you happy?

List five jobs you think you may be interested in.

1 . . . .

2 . . . .

3 . . . .

4 . . . .

5 . . . .

DREAMING ABOUT YOUR

If you could start any business, what would it be?
Why would you want to start this business?

Did You Know?

Small businesses are sometimes called "Mom and Pop" stores.

MAKING MONEY
word scramble

Unscramble each word. Then use the key to unscramble the hidden phrase.

1. nterrreepenu ⑤ ☐☐☐☐☐☐☐☐☐☐☐☐

2. ebdti darc ☐☐☐☐① ☐☐☐☐

3. kecch ☐⑦☐☐☐

4. caeghr ☐☐☐④☐☐

5. essccus ☐②☐☐☐☐☐

6. bkna ☐☐⑧☐

7. nsssubei ☐☐☐☐☐☐☐☐

8. rcaree ☐⑨☐☐☐☐

9. asev ☐☐☐☐

10. npyne ☐☐☐☐⑥

11. llrdoa ☐☐☐⑩☐☐

12. emnoy ⑪☐③☐☐

☐☐☐   ☐☐☐☐   ☐☐☐   ☐☐☐☐☐ ,
① ⑦ ⑤   ⑪ ③ ④ ⑤   ⑥ ③ ②   ⑩ ⑤ ⑨ ④ ⑧

☐☐☐   ☐☐☐☐   ☐☐☐   ☐☐☐☐
① ⑦ ⑤   ⑪ ③ ④ ⑤   ⑥ ③ ②   ⑤ ⑨ ④ ⑧

ANSWER KEY ON PAGE 55

24

Entrepreneur **kids**

JOBS FOR *young* ENTREPRENEURS

You can start your own business right now. In some cases, you may need an adult to help or supervise, but there are plenty of opportunities for you to start your very own business. Here are some different business ideas for kids that might appeal to you.

❶ The Classic Lemonade Stand with a Twist

Open up a lemonade stand! You don't just have to sell lemonade. You could also sell water, low-sugar drinks, and healthy snacks! Reed Floren from Business Success Systems was an entrepreneur from an early age. As a kid, he sold soda, candy, and even the pickle slices from his cheeseburgers. Between the ages of 13-19, Floren was earning $10–20 a day selling snacks to his friends over lunch breaks.

To start his business, he'd buy a six-pack of soda for a couple dollars and then sell each one for $1 apiece. Floren then used the profits to fund buying candy. "I always had plenty of spending money when we went on field trips. If other students needed a loan, I could give them a few bucks and most of them paid me back the very next day," he says.

You can do something similar! On hot days, buy a case of water and sell individual water bottles for $1 each. If you put them in a cooler filled with ice so the water is nice and cold, you may get more business than you think!

Keep Reading! ⟶

LEMONADE STAND

LEMONADE 50¢

❷ Be a Landscape Artist
(a Fancy Term for Mowing Lawns!)

You can find lawn-mowing customers by knocking on doors to see if anyone wants you to mow their lawn. If mowing lawns isn't your thing, you could also ask your neighbors if they'd like you to pull weeds, plant flowers, or water their lawns.

In a few states, there is a company called GreenPal, an app that shows people who want to have their lawn mowed. According to CEO Bryan Clayton: "Many of our lawn care vendors are high school kids and college kids that use our app in the summer to make extra money. Many younger vendors work afternoons and weekends using our app, and it is the perfect way for them to make extra money." On top of that, Bryan said the average GreenPal kid makes around $55 per hour mowing lawns through its app-based system. Kids can set their own hours and pick their clients.

❸ Content Creator

You can create your own content. **Content** is anything creative you make and share online: videos, blogs, websites, art, or even podcasts and apps. If you have a mobile phone or other device with a camera, you can create your own short videos or post pictures of your artwork. "We try to encourage our two teenage daughters to spend time creating their own stuff," Lee Hills, founder of MrExplainer.com, says.

He says his daughters don't have any money to show for their efforts just yet, but he's trying to help them be creative and make content for their own enjoyment.

Did You Know?

The most productive day of the week is Tuesday.

4 Babysit

Do you love little kids? Try babysitting! You can offer to watch your younger brother or sister while the adults run errands or you can offer to babysit for friends and family. If babysitting is not for you, you could also try pet sitting. If your neighbor has a dog, ask them if you can walk their dog. You could also offer to watch their pet while they are out of town.

5 Sell Something You Make

Are you really good at painting pottery or making lip balms or bath bombs? Selling things that you make is a great way to earn some extra money. Thirteen-year-old Lilia ten Bosch of Fremont, CA started her own online business selling homemade lip scrubs, soaps, bath and shower bombs, and lip gloss. She began her business by emailing friends and family to see if anyone was interested in buying them. After getting positive results, she opened up her own Esty store and began making more offering different flavors and scents.

Did You Know?

One in 18 people own their own business!

Keep Reading! →

SELL SOMETHING YOU MAKE

❻ Live Performing Artist

In addition to earning money from a lemonade stand, Rachel Hernandez puts on puppet shows for the community. "Food and entertainment, whether it be for adults or kids, will always draw a crowd and serve the community," she says, adding that most people want to support local businesses.

What makes her puppet shows a success? She says people support her because they know her and she knows their kids. "Plus, I made the extra effort to talk to people. If you can get to know others and they get to know you, you'll have a steady stream of customers to last a lifetime," she adds.

❼ Bottle and Can Collector

Recycling bottles and cans is another great way to earn some extra money. You can collect bottles and cans from your own house or you can collect cans and bottles from other people (be sure to ask them before you do it). Empty aluminum cans and plastic and glass bottles are worth $0.05-0.10 each.

Recycling companies will pay you a fee for all the goods you bring to them, and if you're worried about how you're going to transport all this stuff to them, you can ask a family member for a ride.

❽ T-Shirt Designer

Do you love art and design? If so, it's time to consider becoming a t-shirt designer. These days, through companies like Zazzle, Redbubble, Cafepress, and Spreadshirt, you can get your creative t-shirt designs in front of a huge audience. These services handle all the printing and shipping. All you have to do is create a design that will sell.

By the age of 12, Isabella Rose Taylor had already sewn up an impressive accomplishment. It was one that even some of the most seasoned fashion designers would covet—selling her own collection at the famous department store Nordstrom. The Austin, Texas, native's pieces range from crop tops to graphic tees, mostly in black, white, and grey. Those that feature patterns are inspired by her love of art.

9 Social Media Consultant

Today, most kids know more about social media than their parents. This puts you in a good position to become a social media consultant. As a young person growing up in the Internet age, you have a serious advantage over many adults. You can assist others with setting up and running their social networks, websites, and blogs. Companies pay good money for those with expertise in these areas, and there are plenty of kids who make a great living as social media consultants.

Did You Know?

Someone who is a "jack-of-all-trades" is someone who is good at many things.

10 Personal Assistant to Friends and Family (for a fee)

The busier people are due to their fast-paced lifestyles and careers, the more they hate running errands. You can start a business to run errands for them. For instance, you can pick up groceries, take a dog to the vet, mail packages, or walk younger kids to school or to a friend's house.

You need to be a jack-of-all-trades to be a personal assistant and willing to help with everyday tasks. Think about who needs help in your community: seniors, families, and busy parents. You might also want to think about offering a senior citizens discount to get your foot in the door, or even work for free for the first few jobs to spread the word about your services.

PERSONAL ASSISTANT

Brainstorm Your Money-making Idea

What materials will you need?

....
....
....

What will you sell?

....
....
....

My money-making idea is...

....

Who will work with you?

....
....
....

When will you do your work?

....
....
....
....

Where will you do your business?

....
....
....
....

THE MONEY-MAKING *plan*

All successful businesses start with an idea and a plan. Having a money-making plan is important because it helps keep you organized so that your business can be successful. There are five main parts to a money-making plan.

① Describe Your Money-making Idea

What kind of business do you want to start? Do you think there is a need for this business? How long do you think your business will last? Will people benefit from your business?

② Explain the Need For Your Business

How is your business going to be different from other businesses? How is it the same? If someone else has the same business as you, how are you going to make yours better?

③ Research Your Competition

Think of any businesses that are like the one you want to start. Make a list of them. These businesses will be your competition so you need to know why they are successful or not. What do you like about them? What don't you like about them? Some competition is good, but you don't want to copy someone exactly. Think of ways you can make your business better than ones that are similar.

④ Describe Your Product

Think about what you are selling or creating. If you are looking for an investor, like a family member, you need to have a detailed description of what you are selling. Explain how you are going to make your product. What kinds of things will you need? How are you going to make money?

⑤ Explain How Your Idea Will Work

In this section, explain how the business will work. Will you have any help? What are things you will need to do? Will you need supplies in order to get started? If so, what kinds of supplies? How much money will you need to start your business? How much money do you think you will make?

SAMPLE MONEY-MAKING *plan*

❶ Describe Your Money-Making Idea

My money-making idea is going to be a lemonade stand.

❷ Explain the Need For Your Business

Yes, there is a need for my business because people are thirsty when it's hot outside. I think this business will last for the summer. My lemonade will give people something cold to drink on hot days.

❸ Research Your Competition

I don't have any competition in my neighborhood. The only competition I have is that people could buy lemonade from the grocery store. My lemonade will be freshly squeezed, and I will keep it cold.

❹ Describe Your Product

I am making my own lemonade with lemons from our tree in the backyard. I will also need sugar and ice. If I sell a lot of lemonade and run out of lemons in the backyard, I will need to either ask a neighbor if I can pick their lemons or I will need to buy them from the store.

❺ Explain How Your Idea Will Work

My dad is going to help me build a lemonade stand out of some leftover wood that we have in the garage. I'm going to paint it bright yellow and I'm going to add flowers around it. I will make a big sign so people will know what I'm selling.

WRITE YOUR OWN MONEY-MAKING *plan*

1 Describe **Your Money-Making Idea**

2 Explain the Need **For Your Business**

3 Research Your Competition

4 Describe Your Product

5 Explain How **Your Idea Will Work**

What Is a Profit?

A **profit** is how much money you make after costs when you sell something. For example, if you sell a dozen homemade cookies for $5 and the cost of your ingredients was $10, you didn't make a profit because it cost you more money to make the cookies than it did for you to sell them. If you sell a dozen cookies for $10, and it cost you $5 to make them, then your profit would be $5.

Figure It Out!

I want to sell some bracelets that I made, but I don't know what to charge people for them. How do I figure out how much to charge so I make money?

First, you need to know how much it will cost you to make a bracelet. Here's a sample cost breakdown:

Supplies	**Different colored rubber bands and bracelet maker**
Cost of Supplies	**$10**
How many bracelets can you make from your initial supplies?	**20**
Cost Per Bracelet	**$0.50**

Now that you know how much it costs to make each bracelet, how much should you charge? Do some research to find out how much a similar bracelet costs if you buy it at a store. This is called "checking out the competition." If similar bracelets are sold for

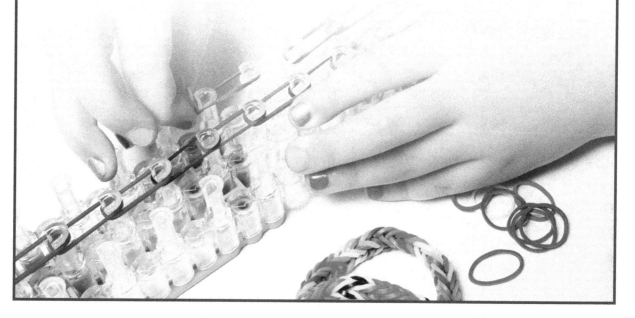

$2, then you know what the competition is charging.

When you own your own business, there usually isn't someone telling you how much you have to charge. Think about what's fair to charge and how much you think people are willing to pay. Plus, you want to make a profit, so don't under charge for your product. If you were to match the competition and sell your bracelets for $2, you would be making a profit of $1 per bracelet. Let's break that down to see how much you would profit if you sold all 20 bracelets.

Total amount earned	$40 ($2 x 20 bracelets)
Minus the cost of supplies	$10
Total profit for 20 bracelets sold	$30

Congratulations! You just made a profit of $30.00!

Make a Plan!

I have a great idea for a business, but I don't know how to get started. What should I do first?

Having an idea is the first step to starting your own business. Then, research! There is a ton of information out there on how to start a business. You should also talk to your parents and get their opinion. They may have some great ideas on how you can get started.

Spread the Word!

How do I get the word out about my new business?

Marketing is sharing information about your business with the community and customers. If you have your own social media account,

Keep Reading! ⟶

post about your business. The best way to get more business is by word of mouth so you want to try to reach as many people as possible. Tell your friends and family. Offer one-time deals or free shipping. You can also hand out flyers to your neighbors.

Name It!

Does the name of my business matter?

Of course it does! There are many factors that should go into the name of your company. First, you don't want to copy someone else. If you wanted to start your own restaurant, do you think you could call it McDonald's? Definitely not. For your first business, make it simple. For example, if your name is Riley and you want to start a dog-walking company, call it: "Riley's Dog-Walking Service." It's simple and to the point. However, if Riley also wants to pet sit, then she should call her business something that isn't just about dog walking. Maybe

something like, "Riley's Dog-Walking and Pet-Sitting Service." Be creative when coming up with the name of your business, but also make sure it's easy to identify what it is.

Find That Money!

I want to start a business, but I don't have any money to get started. What should I do?

Starting any business requires money—some more than others. First, you need to know exactly how much money you need. Then, you could try saving money you get from an allowance or from holidays and birthdays. If starting your own business is going to cost a lot of money, you should probably talk to your parents or grandparents. Before you ask them for a loan (you should pay them back once you start to make money), you should put together a business plan so they can see you're serious about your business. Ⓚ

Find the words that are hidden in the puzzle. Words may be forward, backward, horizontal, vertical, or diagonal.

```
E  J  U  D  R  J  X  R  M  Y  U  E
G  S  E  W  U  V  O  A  H  O  L  D
E  Z  A  H  E  E  R  B  J  C  D  U
L  G  S  U  N  K  G  V  Y  N  E  C
L  C  A  R  E  E  R  C  Z  A  S  A
O  Y  R  T  R  V  E  S  I  I  I  T
C  E  I  Z  P  R  I  M  P  O  G  I
J  N  C  H  E  C  K  T  O  Z  N  O
G  O  G  V  R  U  A  K  A  C  T  N
H  M  A  H  T  B  Y  U  A  E  N  W
M  O  M  A  N  D  P  O  P  N  R  I
D  D  S  S  E  N  I  S  U  B  I  C
```

ENTREPRENEUR	JOB	CAREER	INCOME
MOM AND POP	BUSINESS	MARKETING	CREATIVE
MONEY	RECYCLE	CHECK	
COLLEGE	EDUCATION	DESIGN	

ANSWER KEY ON PAGE 56

MEET THE ENTREPRENEURS:
Lily Brown AND *Tait Hansen*

It doesn't take long to realize why **Lily Brown** and **Tait Hansen** clicked as friends and business partners. The two 13-year-olds love to chat with each other and successfully completed a years-long—and often long-distance—process of creating and designing their own board game.

The result of their efforts, *Betcha Can't!* (originally called *Bet You Can't*), did more than entertain friends and relatives. The game invites players to see who can remember the most trivial information on a subject (like different types of vegetables or modes of transport) in a certain amount of time. It won a share of the grand prize for "Most Marketable Concept" at 2018's Young Inventor Challenge, part of the annual Chicago Toy and Game Week.

Contest sponsor Pressman Toy Corporation quickly picked up the game and worked with Lily and Tait to modify some aspects and prepare it for mass release. As of spring 2020, *Betcha Can't!* has been available nationwide via the original contest's other sponsor, Target.

We talked with Lily and Tait about their money-making idea and how they created *Betcha Can't!*

When did you realize you had an idea for a board game?

Tait: We play-tested it with my family, and it clicked to me when everybody seemed to be having so much fun and no one had played a game like it before.

Lily: Same. All the compliments we were getting were like, "Girls, this is so fun. We love it. It's gonna be a winner!" And that's when I realized, oh, this really could win.

What was the balance between asking your parents for help and designing the game yourselves?

Lily: My dad invents games, so we didn't try to look to him too much, because we really wanted to come up with it on our own. So if we did win and people were like, "Your dad made games, he probably helped you," we could be like, "No, we did it all by ourselves."

Tait: Yeah, I wanted it to feel like our game only and didn't want to feel like we had so much help from adults. But since we were so young when we started it, we did need help a little bit, but for the most part, it was pretty independent.

Is there anything about developing the game you may have done differently?

Tait: Since we started the game in third grade, I would have kept going then instead of dropping the idea of making a game for two years. Because by now, we could have made multiple games.

Lily: Yeah, I agree. I think it would have been good if we just believed in the game right when we made it.

Once Pressman got involved, what was some of the constructive feedback they had?

Lily: When we first made the game, we had a board and we heard the board was too long or didn't really feel like it was interacting as much.

Keep Reading! ⟶

"I wanted it to feel like our game only and didn't want to feel like we had so much help from adults."

Lily Brown (L) and **Tait Hansen** (R)

Tait: Yeah, I remember when we were first told that, we were like, "Oh, this is our game. We wanna keep it how we designed it." But when we play-tested it for the first time without the board, we realized it wasn't really necessary.

Do you think you'll pull off another collaborative project like this despite the distance between you?
Tait: I'd like to make another game with Lily, but I don't have any specific plans. I'm just kind of figuring stuff out right now.
Lily: Same. I think we'd enjoy making another game together.

"I think we'd enjoy making another game together."

Lily and Tait's game, **Betcha Can't!**, was published by Pressman Games and is now on sale at Target.

Have you always been ambitious?
Tait: When we'd hang out with each other, we'd try to make a lot of different businesses when we were younger, so I feel like our minds might have worked a little differently. We didn't really enjoy dressing up as princesses.
Lily: Yeah, we made a massage chair with totally random materials around the house, like straws and popsicle sticks and ping-pong balls and glued them all together and said, "Look, this is a massager!" At one point we even hung fliers around the neighborhood and were like, "We have a business now." We were probably 8 or 9. We didn't get any customers, but we thought we were gonna be super-successful.

Now that you've gotten this early taste of the business world, what do you think?
Tait: I didn't really know what it was like, and I was expecting it to be so much more serious. But it's not really like that. Everyone loves what they do. It was a lot more fun than I was expecting.
Lily: Yeah, when we were in interviews, people weren't uptight and stuff. They were just asking us fun questions.

Do people need to play *Betcha Can't!* by the rules to enjoy it, or do you want people to just have a good time with it in whatever way works for them?
Lily: I found this random YouTube channel with this couple playing our game, but just with the cards and not really playing it and one-upping each other.
Tait: I'm just happy people can interpret the rules however. I don't really mind if they're not playing it exactly how we meant it to be played. As long as they're having fun with it, I'm fine with that. ⓚ

money maze

Jack lost his money.
Help him get through the maze to find it!

ANSWER KEY ON PAGE 56

ALL ABOUT MONEY

MONEY *Lessons* FROM KID ENTREPRENEURS

Entrepreneurs come in all shapes and sizes. As long as you have a passion for success, anyone can create their own business and bring their vision to life. And there are a handful of kids who are making their presence in the entrepreneurial world known.

These kid entrepreneurs range from 8- to 18-years-old but already understand how to run their own businesses and how to manage their money. Here are five young entrepreneurs with some valuable tips on ways to make good choices about your money.

❶ Asking for Money Isn't Always the Answer

When Moziah Bridges founded his handmade bowtie business, Mo's Bows, at the age of nine, he began with just three employees: his mother, his grandmother, and himself. Since starting Mo's Bows, Bridges has sold more than $300,000 worth of bowties and men's accessories, catching the eye of his current mentor, Daymond John. After appearing on the television show *Shark Tank* with his mother, John told Bridges to turn down any money offers for his business and to continue growing Mo's Bows on his own. The lesson? Sometimes it's better for a business owner to grow their company slowly rather than to hand over ownership in exchange for short-term money.

❷ If You Don't Love Your Job, It's Not Worth It

Part of starting your own business is chasing your dreams and seeing your vision come to life; often times, money isn't the main goal for entrepreneurs. Ollie Forsyth found his passion for entrepreneurship running his own online boutique and runs a charity that supports young entrepreneurs in school. And while Forsyth makes good money from his online shop, he's less interested in profit and focused on giving back to others and having fun running his business. As the young entrepreneur puts it, "There's no point in earning millions if you hate your job."

❸ Have Responsibility for the Environment Around You

Mikaila Ulmer was stung by a bee at just 4 years old, which began her fascination with bees and inspired her honey-sweetened lemonade recipe. She founded Me & The Bees Lemonade. Since her appearance on *Shark Tank*, Ulmer received an $11 million-dollar deal with 55 Whole Foods stores across the nation who will now carry her signature drink. But don't think Ulmer's focus is just about making a profit.

Keep Reading! ⟶

> ## "There's no point in earning millions if you hate your job."

Ulmer donates a portion of her profits to local and international organizations fighting to save honeybees. In business, it's not always about making as much money as possible.

④ Build Around a Need in Your Life

Sometimes a business is born out a specific necessity. For Rachel Zietz, she found her business in the form of lacrosse practice equipment and her company, Gladiator Lacrosse is on track to make $1 to $2 million dollars.

Zietz's idea was simple: As a varsity lacrosse player, she and her fellow teammates needed sturdier, high-quality practice equipment that current manufacturers couldn't deliver. The market for lacrosse equipment is roughly $100 million and Zietz has found herself a unique niche. Entrepreneurs don't need to have a big crazy idea to be successful; just like Zietz's Gladiator Lacrosse, a business that meets a specific need in a niche market can lead to a profitable idea.

⑤ Use Local Sources to Reduce Costs

At only eight years old, Mia Felber has been able to create a business that makes 100-percent natural pet care products for pets called Paleo Pets. Her idea came while trying to find natural products for her own pets. Following in her mother's footsteps, she figured out how to create healthy and safe products for cats and dogs using local ingredients. As an entrepreneur, finding the right ingredients for your product can be expensive. To cut down on cost, Mia looked to local sources for their ingredients.

You're never too young to pursue your goals and many of these kid entrepreneurs have proven that age is just a number. Sometimes the simplest ideas are the best ideas, and learning to budget finances early on can help you grow your business in the long-run. ⓚ

saving MONEY

Make It a Habit

Saving is one of the most important things you can ever do with money. As fun as it can be to spend money, saving money and watching it grow into more money will set your future self up for success. When you receive money, you should get in the habit of automatically saving a portion. How much should you save?

A good rule of thumb is 20 percent. If grandma gives you $50 for your birthday, you should automatically save $10. There's nothing wrong with saving more than that. In fact, if you can save more, then you should. The more money you save, the more money you'll have.

Keep Reading! ⟶

SAVINGS *goals*

What are your savings goals? You should have two kinds of goals—big ones and little ones. Big ones, like saving to buy a car when you're 16 or saving for college, are long-term savings goals. Smaller savings goals, like saving to buy a new backpack or new shoes, are short-term savings goals.

What are three of your long-term savings goals?

1 ....
2 ....
3 ....

What are three of your short-term savings goals?

1 ....
2 ....
3 ....

Long-Term Savings Goals

Long-term saving means you don't want to touch your money for a while. The best place to save this money is in a savings account or a certificate of deposit (CD) account. If you don't already have a savings account, you will need to ask your parents to go with you to the bank to open one. A regular **savings account** is a safe place to put your money. Banks will pay you interest to keep your money there. The interest won't be very much, but it can add up over time.

A **CD account** is similar to a savings account. The biggest difference is that you will have to keep your money in the account for a certain amount of time. The amount of time can vary depending on the type of CD account. For example, it may be for three years or five years. Why would you want to open up a CD account? Because the interest that the bank gives you is more than it is for a regular savings account, which means you'll make more money.

Let's say you want to save enough money to buy a used car when you are 16. The car will cost about $5,000. Today, you are 11.

Long-term savings goal (5 years to save)	$5,000
Amount needed to save each year for the next 5 years	$1,000
Amount needed to save each month for the next 5 years	**$84**

Do you think you can save $84 a month?
Why? Or why not?

Short-Term Savings Goals

You don't usually need to put the money you save for short-term goals in the bank. You could save this money in a piggy bank or a jar in your bedroom. Beware, though! Sometimes saving for short-term goals is more difficult than it is for long-term goals because the money is easier for you to access and spend. K

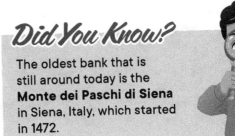

Did You Know?

The oldest bank that is still around today is the **Monte dei Paschi di Siena** in Siena, Italy, which started in 1472.

Six-Month Savings Challenge

WEEK	AMOUNT	TOTAL	WEEK	AMOUNT	TOTAL
Week 1	$0.75	**$0.75**	Week 14	$4.00	**$33.25**
Week 2	$1.00	**$1.75**	Week 15	$4.25	**$37.50**
Week 3	$1.25	**$3.00**	Week 16	$4.50	**$42.00**
Week 4	$1.50	**$4.50**	Week 17	$4.75	**$46.75**
Week 5	$1.75	**$6.25**	Week 18	$5.00	**$51.75**
Week 6	$2.00	**$8.25**	Week 19	$5.25	**$57.00**
Week 7	$2.25	**$10.50**	Week 20	$5.50	**$62.50**
Week 8	$2.50	**$13.00**	Week 21	$5.75	**$68.25**
Week 9	$2.75	**$15.75**	Week 22	$6.00	**$74.25**
Week 10	$3.00	**$18.75**	Week 23	$6.25	**$80.50**
Week 11	$3.25	**$22.00**	Week 24	$6.50	**$87.00**
Week 12	$3.50	**$25.50**	Week 25	$6.75	**$93.75**
Week 13	$3.75	**$29.25**	Week 26	$7.25	**$101.00!**

DREAMING ABOUT
saving

How much money would you like to save by the time you graduate from high school? What do you hope to do with that money?

budgeting 101

Budgeting is creating a plan so you don't spend more money than you have. To create a budget, first pay attention to how much you earn. If it's different every week or month, you may need to do this for a couple months to give you an idea of how much money you are bringing in. Also pay attention to how much you spend. Keep track of all of your receipts. Put them in a special box for safe keeping. Then at the end of the week, add up all of your receipts to see how much money you spent and on what. 🄺

My Budget

How much money I make every month $ ....

What I plan to spend each month

Eating out: $ ....

Shopping: $ ....

Activities: $ ....

Miscellaneous: $ ....

What I plan to save each month

Short-term savings: $ ....

Long-term savings: $ ....

SAVING
smarts

What's a Deposit?
A **deposit** is an amount of money that you are putting into your bank account. Each time you put money into your savings account, you are depositing money into that account.

How Do You Withdraw Money from a Bank?
A **withdrawal** is when you take money out of your account. If you need to take money out of your savings account, you are withdrawing the money.

How Much Money Can You Get from an ATM?
An **ATM** is an automatic teller machine that dispenses money to you from your bank account when you insert your debit card and enter a secret code known as a PIN. How much you can get depends on how much money you have and it also depends on how much money the bank sets as the daily limit. Most banks won't let you take out more than $500-$1000 per day. The limits are put in place for safety reasons. However, you also have to have money in your account in order to use the ATM. If you only have $100 in savings, you can't go to the ATM and take more than that.

Keep Reading! ⟶

ALL ABOUT MONEY

What Does It Mean to Borrow Money?

Borrowing money means someone is giving you money with the expectation that you are going to pay them back. For example, if you want to buy a new phone case and it costs $30, but you only have $25, how are you going to come up with the rest of the money? You could wait until you have all of the money or you could borrow it. If you ask your mom to lend you the $5 until your next allowance, that means when you get your next allowance, it will be $5 less because of the money you owed.

It is important to understand that borrowing money doesn't mean you have more money; it means you have the use of it.

When things cost a lot of money like a car or a house or going to college, many people borrow money. When you borrow money from a bank, they will charge you interest, which means you will end up paying more than the actual borrowed amount.

Cost of Car	**$10,000**
Amount of Time to Pay Off	**3 years**
Interest Rate	**6%**
Monthly Payment	**$304.22**
Total Amount Paid to Lender	**$10,951.92**

If you had taken out this loan, you would have had to pay $951.92 more than you borrowed—this is one way that banks make money.

money fun

Molly wants to build a treehouse. She needs $10 for wood and nails. She decides to recycle plastic bottles and cans to earn money. One pound of recycled plastic bottles is worth $1.28 and one pound of recycled cans is worth $1.65. Help Molly sort out the plastic bottles and cans to see if she has enough money to build the treehouse.

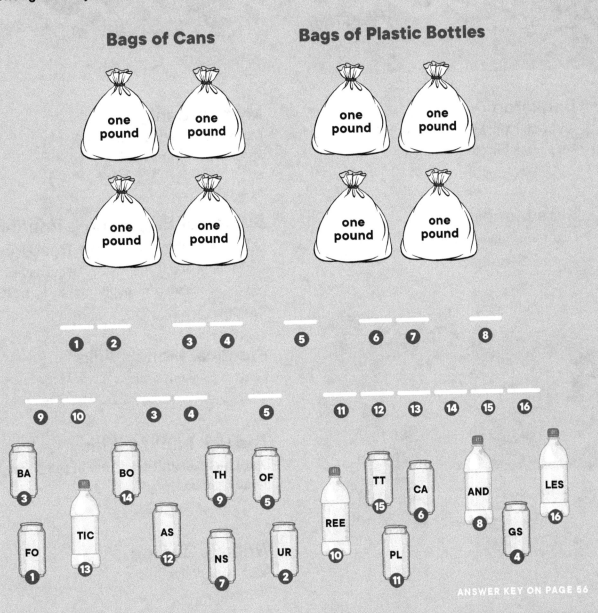

ANSWER KEY ON PAGE 56

MONEY
resources

Bankaroo

A virtual bank for kids where you can virtually keep track of your allowance.

■ bankaroo.com

Kid's Money

Learn more about making money.

■ kidsmoney.org

My Kids Bank

Learn about money management by creating an artificial online bank.

■ mykidsbank.org

Bureau of Engraving & Printing
U.S. Department of the Treasury

Learn more about the history of currency and watch videos on how paper money is made!

■ moneyfactory.gov

Practical Money Skills

Fun games about money.

■ practicalmoneyskills.com/play

The U.S. Mint for Kids

Learn more about the history of coins and play money games.

■ usmint.gov/learn/kids

Where's George

Track your dollar bills!

■ wheresgeorge.com

puzzle solutions

Match The Money page 12

China: D, France: G, Japan: F, Mexico: B,
Nigeria: A, Serbia: E, United Kingdom: C

Word Search page 13

```
C W N W C B J Y O C Y N
J R A I D H R S U O O B
E G E P L A A R M I T A
E T W D L K R S T S R R
O M O A I E N A E D A T
R D S N N T N A V E D E
A X S C Q I C I R A E R
L Z Y F M U E A Y F H I
L A M O N E Y N R F V N
O O N I O C O H D D E G
D E I F N O T L I M A H
D N U M I S M A T I S T
```

Crossword page 17

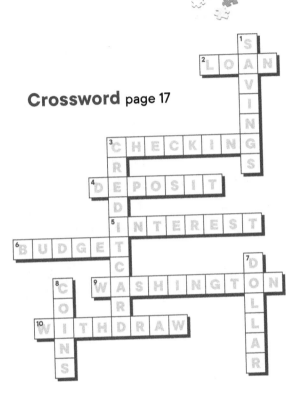

Word Scramble page 24

1. entrepreneur
2. debit card
3. check
4. charge
5. success
6. bank
7. business
8. career
9. save
10. penny
11. dollar
12. money

THE (1)(7)(5) MORE (11)(3)(4)(5) YOU (6)(3)(2) LEARN (10)(5)(9)(4)(8) ,

THE (1)(7)(5) MORE (11)(3)(4)(5) YOU (6)(3)(2) EARN (5)(9)(4)(8)

puzzle solutions

Word Search page 37

```
E J U D R J X R M Y U E
G S E W U V O A H O L D
E Z A H E E R B J C D U
L G S U N K G V N E E C
L C A R E E R C Z A S A
O Y R T R V E S I I I T
C E I Z P R I M P O G I
J N C H E C K T O Z N O
G O G V R U A K A C T N
H M A H T B Y U A E N W
M O M A N D P O P N R I
D D S S E N I S U B I C
```

Money Maze page 41

Money Fun page 53

FO UR   BA GS   OF   CA NS   AND
① ②   ③ ④   ⑤   ⑥ ⑦   ⑧

TH REE   BA GS   OF   PL AS TIC BO TT LES
⑨ ⑩   ③ ④   ⑤   ⑪ ⑫ ⑬ ⑭ ⑮ ⑯

CPSIA information can be obtained
at www.ICGtesting.com
Printed in the USA
JSHW021513070221
11526JS00002B/5